Mommy, Daddy
Please Teach Me!

Written by Michael A. Brown   Illustrated by Zoe Ranucci

This book is dedicated to...

Parents, Guardians, Caregivers, and Children alike. What you will read herein are things I'd tell my mom that got me into trouble. Well, what we don't learn as children create vacuums of insecurity that we ignore as adults because we depend on others to do what we should know how to do. What you teach your child NOW will secure their insecurities, show them they are loved through the action of teaching, and that they belong to themselves first and to a family unit.
Get to reading. You all have work to do.

First Edition

Edited by Michele L. Mathews

Illustration by Zoe Ranucci

Design by Zoe Ranucci, www.GoodDharma.com

ISBN: 978-1-7352024-7-1

Library of Congress Control Number: 2020918427

You gave me life. Now I am here

For who knows how many years.

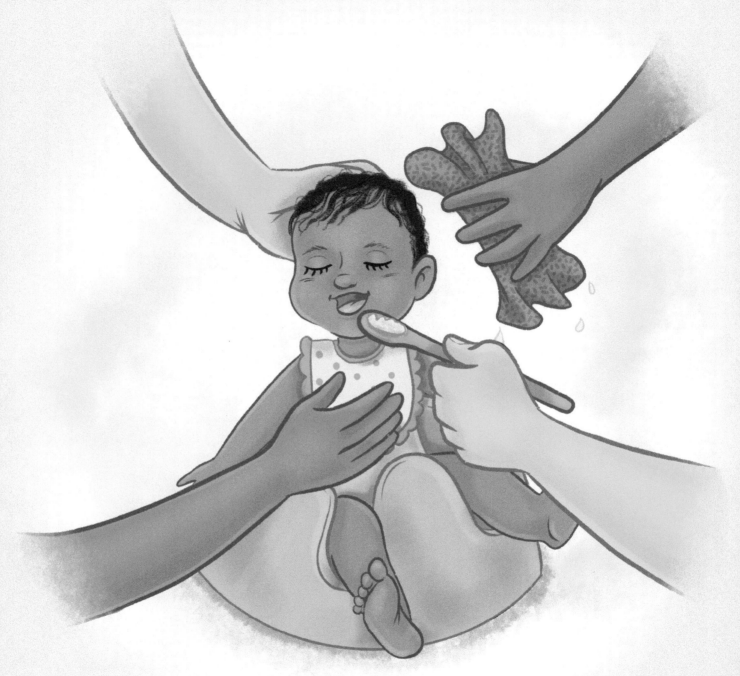

You give me love by what you do.

Protect, clean, and feed me, too.

You played with me and watched me crawl.

Now I walk. I'm standing tall.

More alert, I look to thee.
Mommy, Daddy, please teach me!

Don't just clothe me; teach me how
To dress my best for years from now.

A family, I may have
With boys and girls, ties and pearls.

Comb their hair?
Cut it, too?

Maybe a dress?
What size of shoes?

How do I know
what to choose?

Teach me how
so I don't lose.

Don't just cook; teach me how
I'll need to feed myself somehow.

A family, I'll have someday

To cook for them a million ways.

In the store, I see food.
Veggies and fruits, so much to choose.

How much money does that cost?

Don't just spend; teach me, boss!

Dollars, pennies,
nickels, and dimes.

Teach me money!

We've got the time.

Now we're home. Yes, where we stay.
Can I put the food away?

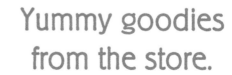

Yummy goodies
from the store.

Look! A spill on the floor!

Don't just clean; can I mop, too?
Teach me how to clean like you!

A clean house, I'll need to keep
To beautify where I shall sleep.

Have a job or a career?
Work every day of the year?

Don't just work; teach me how!
You make money for me somehow.

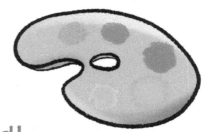

A skill or trade, I will need!

Soon my job to do for me.

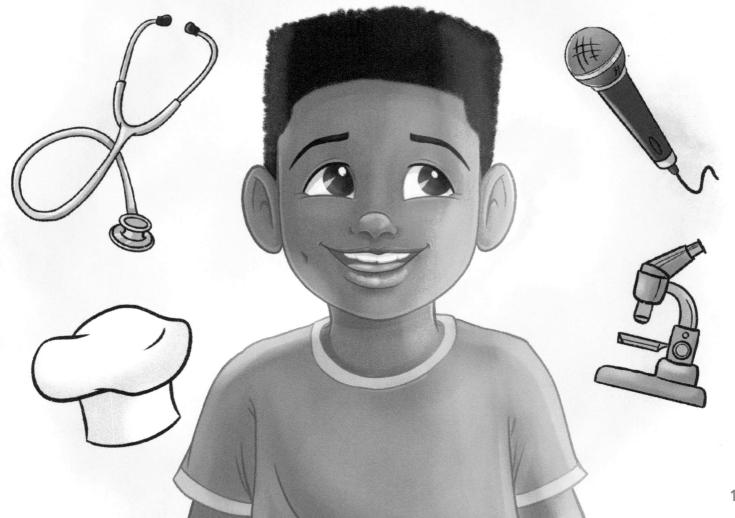

Going somewhere?
Don't just run.

Take me with!
**Teach me
what's fun!**

Just all work and no play?

Teach me to live life away.

ABCs and 123s
I can say these with great ease.

Don't stop there; please teach me
All about my self-esteem.

What should I tell myself first?

I can be great! I love me FIRST!

I know I must do for me

That which makes me so happy.

I sure learned a lot today.
Mom and Dad just taught away.

Teach me now the way to go.

I love you both. Now watch me grow.

27

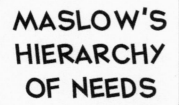

MASLOW'S HIERARCHY OF NEEDS

ABRAHAM MASLOW

MORALITY, CREATIVITY, SPONTANEITY, PROBLEM SOLVING, LACK OF PREJUDICE, ACCEPTANCE OF FACTS

SELF-ACTUALIZATION

SELF-ESTEEM, CONFIDENCE, ACHIEVEMENT, RESPECT OF OTHERS, RESPECT BY OTHERS

ESTEEM

FRIENDSHIP, FAMILY ASSOCIATIONS, ACTIVITIES

LOVE/BELONGING

SECURITY OF BODY, OF EMPLOYMENT, OF RESOURCES, OF MORALITY, OF THE FAMILY, OF HEALTH, OF PROPERTY

SAFETY

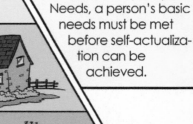

BREATHING, FOOD, WATER, SLEEP, HOMEOSTASIS, EXCRETION

PHYSIOLOGICAL

Abraham Harold Maslow (April 1, 1908 - June 8, 1970) was a psychologist who studied positive human qualities and the lives of exemplary people. In 1954, Maslow created the Hierarchy of Human Needs and expressed his theories in his book, <u>Motivation and Personality</u>.

Self-Actualization - A person's motivation to reach his or her full potential. As shown in Maslow's Hierarchy of Needs, a person's basic needs must be met before self-actualization can be achieved.

©Tim van de Vall

About the Author

Born in Chicago, IL, Michael A. (Mike) Brown, MA is the author of a revolutionary social emotional children's book series, What I Tell Myself, beginning with What I Tell Myself FIRST: Children's Real-World Affirmations of Self-Esteem. Based on Maslow's Hierarchy of Needs, this book of real-world affirmations highlights the various abilities and attributes of the reader while exposing readers to realistic possibilities of rejection of difference in various forms thereby enabling readers to form mental frameworks to surmount those forms of rejection and achieve positive self-actualization. Mr. Brown continues the mission to heal and empower all with the What I Tell Myself series of books.

Mr. Brown is a product of the Chicago Public School system. He served in the United States Army and in various communities as a police officer. He is currently the President and Chief Executive Officer of MABMA Enterprises, LLC and the principal instructor of Security Training Concepts, a training agency specializing in collegiate / career occupational courses in multiple criminal justice and self-defense-related disciplines. Mr. Brown also serves as a nationally-certified anger management specialist and Crisis Prevention Institute-certified nonviolent crisis intervention instructor. He is the father of four beautiful children and believes in raising them into the best strong, capable, productive, responsible, and most importantly, happy human beings they can be. A former adjunct college professor and advocate of education, Mr. Brown is a graduate of Governors State University in University Park, Illinois, having been conferred a Bachelor of Arts degree in Interdisciplinary Studies (Criminal Justice, Psychology and Philosophy) in 2006 and a Master of Arts degree in Criminal Justice in 2012. He serves as an innovative and fresh approach to leadership, training, and empowerment and is a member of the International Law Enforcement Educators and Trainers Association, the National Anger Management Association, and the Society of Children's Book Writers and Illustrators.

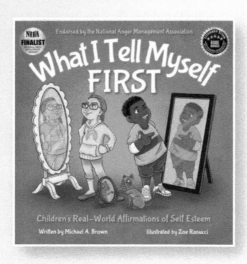

What I Tell Myself FIRST *is on a mission to heal kids and parents! Real-world affirmations WORK!*

Like the AED is to a heart, this book instills the defibrillator of self-esteem. So powerful that it addresses bullying and outside attacks on the self by other people who need the very same help themselves. For when times are tough and your mind is under attack, reality-based daily affirmations are the "I wish I had this" of books.

What I Tell Myself FIRST will help to heal wounds and rejuvenate self-esteem. We MUST instill in our children the answer to bullying, body-shaming, hate, and attacks on the self through daily affirmations.

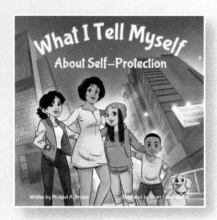

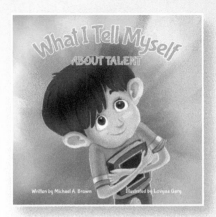

What I Tell Myself About Self—Protection is continuing the mission to heal and empower adults, parents, grandparents, children, caretakers, crime victims, and others inspiring readers to take an active approach to self-protection against active threats and deadly threatening situations.

From declaring one's right to be free and grow to being situationally aware, this book guides readers to take strong decisive actions and empower their loved ones or those in their care to do the same. Whether there's danger head or imminently present, it is NO ONE's job to protect you. It is your job. Be. Know. Do. Survive.

Some are great at some things. Others are good at other things. Some are not good at some things. But, what are your children great, good, or not good at? Some children become adults never having harnessed their inner talents.

That's where **What I Tell Myself About Talent** enters in continuing the mission to heal and empower adults, parents, grandparents, caretakers and other readers in helping children actively explore their current and future talents through everyday things they do. Inner talent recognition is essential for positive self actualization in all children. From performing arts and the trades to selfless-serving occupations, help your child explore their inner talents and guide them toward positive self-actualization. Be. Know. Do. Explore.

www.WhatITellMyselfFirst.com

CPSIA information can be obtained
at www.ICGtesting.com
Printed in the USA
BVHW062124300920
590046BV00001B/2

9 781735 202471